Thank-You Notes to God

a prayer & gratitude journal

STEPHANIE L. JONES

giving gal

Giving Gal Press books may be ordered by contacting Giving Gal Press, a division of Giving Gal, LLC, www.GivingGal.com, 219-707-9545.

ISBN: 978-1-948693-06-6
Library of Congress Control Number: 2021905908

Print information available on the last page.

Cover design by Stephanie L Jones, Rebekah Northern, and Melinda Martin

Giving Gal Press Date April 1, 2021

To Murage,
who taught me the power of writing down your prayers.

And to my sister,
who gave me my first gratitude journal.

Both have changed my life for the better.

Thank-You Notes to God Gives Back

A portion of the proceeds from every copy of *this book* is donated to organizations that support Christian discipleship in students and adults.

Thank you for your support!

Note from the Author

Prayer

I am no expert on prayer. I have not written a book or taken classes in seminary on the topic, but I have been writing my prayers for years. Through documentation, we can physically see the power of our prayers, even when they are not perfect.

I started writing down my prayers in college. I shared with a friend how I tried praying, but within minutes—heck, even seconds—my mind drifted into the deep blue sea, never to return to the prayer I started. My friend recommended I write my prayers to help me focus. To say his advice worked wonders is an understatement.

Over the years, I drifted away from consistently writing my prayers and found myself tossing up prayers on a whim throughout the day. I do not think God cares if we write our prayers or toss them up to Him on a whim. He is our friend—our pen pal, so to speak—and first thing in the morning, during the day, and at the end of the day, He wants to hear from us.

However, I have found I am more in tune with listening to the Holy Spirit when I write my prayers. Ideas flow from the clouds down into my pen.

The last couple of years, I have delved into daily devotionals and the powerful experience of reading through the Bible in a year. Along the way, I reignited writing my prayers. What a gift God has given me as I look back at answered and unanswered prayers, doors opened and closed, and most of all, His faithfulness. As my friend, Emily, reminded me, God is the ultimate gift-giver. The spiritual gifts, grace, and forgiveness He gives us are some of the most valuable gifts of all.

I have read several books that have helped me learn about prayer including *The Power of a Praying Wife* and *The Power of a Praying Woman* by Stormie Omartian, and *Fervent* by Priscilla Shirer.

As I read through these books, I flipped open my Bible, underlined verses, made notes, and pondered what God was speaking to me. Often the silence led to a thought I needed to write about so I would whip out my prayer journal and off I would go in prayer.

Prayer looks different for all of us. If you don't know where to begin, start with the Lord's Prayer found in Matthew 6:8 (NLT).

Our Father in heaven,
May your name be kept holy.
May your Kingdom come soon.
May your will be done on earth,
As it is in heaven.
Give us today the food we need
And forgive us our sins,
As we forgive those who sin against us.
And don't let us yield to temptation,
But rescue us from the evil one.

Gratitude

Years ago, my sister gave me my first gratitude journal. Each day, I write down five things for which I'm grateful. My gratitude list evolved into a daily thank you note to God for all the goodness in my life. These lists are a reminder that we should not just come to Him with a laundry list of requests and confessions, but we should also take a moment to pause and recognize all the good in our lives. I realized by practicing gratitude that, even on hard days, there is always something to be grateful for if we only look for it.

I kicked my gratitude practice into high gear during my giving journey. Beginning January 1, 2011, I gave a gift every day for 522 consecutive days. Giving this way stretched me in gratitude. I found contentment with what I own and where I am in life. I'm happier. Days of depression are few and far between. When I observe my surroundings, I notice beauty in the small things I ignored in the past. Practicing gratitude, which took little time and no money, changed my life.

We, as a society, have trouble focusing on today. But reading the Bible and practicing gratitude teach us to be content where we are in life and with what God has given us. We are less likely to make our happiness dependent on our material possessions or to fear what might happen in the future.

Practicing gratitude will change your perspective on life, especially if you do it consistently.

Why I Created *Thank-You Notes to God*

I created *Thank-You Notes to God* as I found the writing of my prayers and the expression of my gratitude to God intertwined perfectly with one another in a natural flow.

My prayer is that combining prayer and gratitude into one journal will draw us closer to God so that, even in dark times, we can be grateful for each day God gives us.

That's why I designed *Thank You Notes to God* to be a tool in your daily life. If you write in it daily, or at least several times a week, you can go back to your previous entries when you are feeling down or need a boost. You can see all the good days, all the things you have to be grateful for, and all your answered and unanswered prayers. The more you write, the more entries you will have for your times of reflection.

Daily Bible Verse

Start by reading the daily verse.

After that, I encourage you to read the entire chapter for that verse. Ask God to use His word to speak wisdom and truth into your life and open your eyes to areas of sin, change, and forgiveness.

Don't have time to read the entire chapter? That is okay. Use the verse provided as a starting place for your day or the last thing you read before you go to bed. Let the Word of God seep into your mind and soul, providing you guidance, comfort, peace, and joy.

Consider snapping a picture of the verse and sharing it on social media. I am all about spreading positivity and the love of Christ with those we are connected with on social media.

What I Want to Remember Today

The journal includes a section called: "What I want to remember today." I don't know about you, but some events happen in my life that I don't want to forget. The event does not have to be significant. It could be a milestone at work, something funny your child said, or an idea God laid on your heart.

Whatever it is, please take a minute to jot it down. Your future self will thank you.

Today I'm Grateful For...

How much should you write in the gratitude space? That is totally up to you.

You can write in bullet points, complete sentences, or paragraphs. I do recommend striving to write down three to five things you are grateful for daily. One item often seems like an easy task, but three and beyond makes me pause, think about my life, and pay attention to my surroundings.

To provide you with a jump start on gratitude, I have included two stories from my book, *The Gratitude Challenge*, as a bonus:

- I'm Grateful for an Unanswered Prayer, and
- I'm Grateful for Answered Prayers.

If you want to learn more about gratitude, check out this book.

Prayer

Some days my prayers are long; other days, they are short. There is no guidance on how long a prayer must be. Let the words flow from your heart onto the paper.

I have included two full pages in the journal, but do not be intimidated by the space. If you only write a couple of lines, that is okay. If you have extra space, either leave it blank or come back at a later time and journal through unanswered or answered prayers related to that day. This is your journal—use it as you see fit.

Other Resources

Friends often post on social media or send me a text asking for prayers. I am intentional about not responding until after I have prayed. I do not want to forget about the prayer. I scribble my friend's name in my journal and continue to pray until God has answered or given His decision to a prayer.

The journal includes a couple of pages to write down prayer requests so you can remember to incorporate them into your daily prayer time. The list can also prompt you to send a text, a phone call, a note of encouragement, or even a gift.

Let us be intentional about praying for our friends, family, and even strangers.

I also include a list of things to pray for as it would be wonderful for all those that use *Thank-You Notes to God* to be praying powerfully for change in our world. These ideas may give you a jump start on days you struggle to pray.

Thank you for going on this journey with me. May the practice of prayer and gratitude strengthen your relationship with Christ and draw you nearer to Him each day.

The Gratitude Challenge

I'm Grateful for an Unanswered Prayer

After pulling into a gravel driveway, we parked and exited our vehicle. I grabbed my husband's hand, and we trekked thirty-five wooded acres of our dream property. Breathing in, cold-air puddles filled my eyes. I couldn't believe in a few short months this property would be ours. I'd prayed on more than one occasion we would own enough land that I could walk out my back door and be on miles of trails. God answered my prayers, or so I thought. We made an offer, and the seller accepted. Wahoo!

We put down our deposit and waited for the soil test results. Then the unexpected happened. The soil testing failed. We were surprised and devastated. But that devastation quickly turned to gratitude. Our realtor, wise enough to make the sale contingent on a soil test, protected us, so we didn't waste thousands of dollars on unbuildable land.

Six months later, we stumbled on a ten-acre wooded property with a home and a separate garage for my husband's woodworking projects. The house had not been updated since 1988. Another dream bubbled to the surface.

We'd always wanted to remodel a house. We never envisioned it would be a home we were living in, but a home we'd buy and flip or use as a rental. God had other plans.

Once again, we made an offer, contingent on the home inspection. Friends, the home inspection revealed a litany of issues. The biggest?

Mice overrunning the attic and insulation. Yikes! But sometimes, major obstacles can be handled with the right expert. We made a couple of calls, and the rodent guys arrived and shared a plan we could execute. We moved forward.

As of this writing, we are in the throes of an entire home remodel. Box springs with a mattress are set up in the living room. We have no kitchen, and I have the coffee pot in the laundry room. My jobs include hauling trim to the dumpster, removing wallpaper border, and scooting around on my hands and knees, pulling staples out of the floor. I haven't worked this hard in my life. I tell myself that each of these tasks builds mental strength.

I'm grateful for unanswered prayers. I can't fathom where we'd be if we'd purchased the thirty-five acres of bad soil. As my friend Susan said, "Somedays you don't get what you want, but you get what you need."

Gratitude Challenge

What prayer(s) has God answered in your life? ______________________

____

____

____

____

Today I'm grateful for ______________________________________

____

____

____

____

Thank-You Note Challenge

Who was involved in your unanswered prayer? Send a thank-you note to that person. This one may be difficult but therapeutic.

The Gratitude Challenge

I'm Grateful for Answered Prayers

Do you have days when you forget the prayers God answered in your life?

Sometimes we hit a stretch in life when nothing seems to be going our way.

I like writing down my prayers. A college friend gave me the idea when I shared with him that I'd often get lost in thought or distracted when praying. He recommended I write down my prayers, which would help me focus. Twenty years later, I'm still writing down my prayers.

Not only does writing down my prayers keep me focused, but I love going back, reading my prayer requests, and making a note of when God answered a prayer. Many of these answered prayers turn into what I'm thankful for today. Documenting the prayers God answers is helpful when we don't feel like He's heard our current prayers or maybe isn't answering how we think the prayer should be answered.

Here is one prayer I often pray: "Lord protect me. Give me strength. Take away my fear. Please let me go and stay asleep."

In high school, I attended a concert with a friend. When he dropped me off at home, my parents were not there.

I let myself in the house, went to my room, and passed out.

The next morning, rays of light streamed into the room, and I wondered why my blinds were open. I knew they were closed before leaving for the concert.

Sauntering into the living room, I asked my mom why she'd opened my blinds.

"I didn't. We need to chat." My mom's serious response concerned me.

I won't go into all the details, but the gist of the story is the police believe a stranger had been in the house when I came home and entered my room while I slept. By the grace of God, I never woke up through the entire ordeal.

Though I was physically unharmed, that one event wrecked me emotionally and changed my perspective on life and my sense of security. Twenty-five years later, I struggle when I am home alone and often live in fear.

When my husband is not home in the evenings or is away on a work trip, anxiety pours over me like a crashing waterfall. Heck, sometimes, when he is lying beside me in bed, I still have anxiety.

But not every night is a struggle. Here is an entry from April 2, 2017:

> "Mike was at the lake house. I always stay up until I'm completely exhausted. Right before I go to sleep, I ask God to give me protection and to sleep through the night. This morning I woke up at 7:00 a.m. I never sleep this late. God is good."

Every time I read this entry; I am reminded that not all nights when my husband is gone are bad. That I can have a good night's sleep, even if I anticipate not sleeping.

God may not answer all our prayers, but when He does, take note and be grateful.

Gratitude Challenge

What prayer(s) has God answered in your life? ____________

____

____

____

____

Today I'm grateful for ____________________

____

____

____

____

Thank-You Note Challenge

Did God answer a prayer about someone in your life? If so, drop this person a note about why she is important to your life.

People Who Need Prayer

Date	Person	Note

I don't know about you, but sometimes I sit down to pray, and my mind is blank. Maybe I'm weary, just waking up, or feeling down and out. During these times, I listen to what God has to say to me. Over the past year, I have compiled a list of things we can always be praying for as we chat with God.

Better yet, we can expand upon these topics in our prayer journals.

Make these topics specific to the calling on your heart. Can you imagine how our world would change if every believer prayed for these things?

Pray for:

- the hopeless
- those going through trials
- protection of our men and women in the military
- salvation of nonbelievers
- those engaged in spiritual warfare
- women and children trapped in abusive relationships
- victims of sexual assault
- those in the bondage of sin
- drug addicts
- the oppressed
- churches
- injustices in our society
- children who are bullied in school
- families in financial crisis
- the homeless

- those who are lonely
- couples struggling with infertility
- single people who long for a lifelong partner
- marriages
- guidance and direction in life (ourselves and others)
- our enemies
- cancer patients
- healthcare workers
- police officers for both their physical and mental well-being
- those who are grieving the loss of a loved one
- for children who have strayed away from their parents and homes
- missing children
- people we need to forgive
- prisoners in our correctional facilities and the staff that care for them
- pastors and church staff
- community and nonprofit organizations
- our president, vice president, congress, and the supreme court
- our country
- countries around the world
- farmers and abundant crops
- encouragement for those that need it

- financial troubles
- faith when we have doubts
- courage when we are fearful
- rest for a weary soul
- dependence on you, Lord
- discernment of what is true and not true, good versus evil
- addictions to food, sugar, and alcohol
- doors of opportunity to open
- small businesses
- a deeper, stronger faith
- a joyful heart
- contentment with what I have and where I am in life
- my spouse
- my children
- my extended family
- my friends
- strangers that cross my path
- college students
- courage to share the love of Jesus Christ
- peace in our world
- the hungry to be fed and provided fresh clean water
- healing for diseases
- medical breakthroughs
- a good night's sleep

- the ability to say no to the activities that are not serving you, Lord
- the courage to quit busy
- an attitude of gratitude
- a generous heart
- eyes to see people like Christ Jesus does
- anger in my heart to dissipate
- a deeper faith
- humility
- safe travels

Pray in the Spirit
at all times
and on every occasion.
Stay alert
and be persistent
in your prayers
for all believers
everywhere.

Ephesians 6:18

Date:

Today I want to remember:

Today I am grateful for:

Prayer

Every time
I think of you,
I give thanks
to my God.

PHILIPPIANS 1:3

DATE:

TODAY I WANT TO REMEMBER:

TODAY I AM GRATEFUL FOR:

Prayer

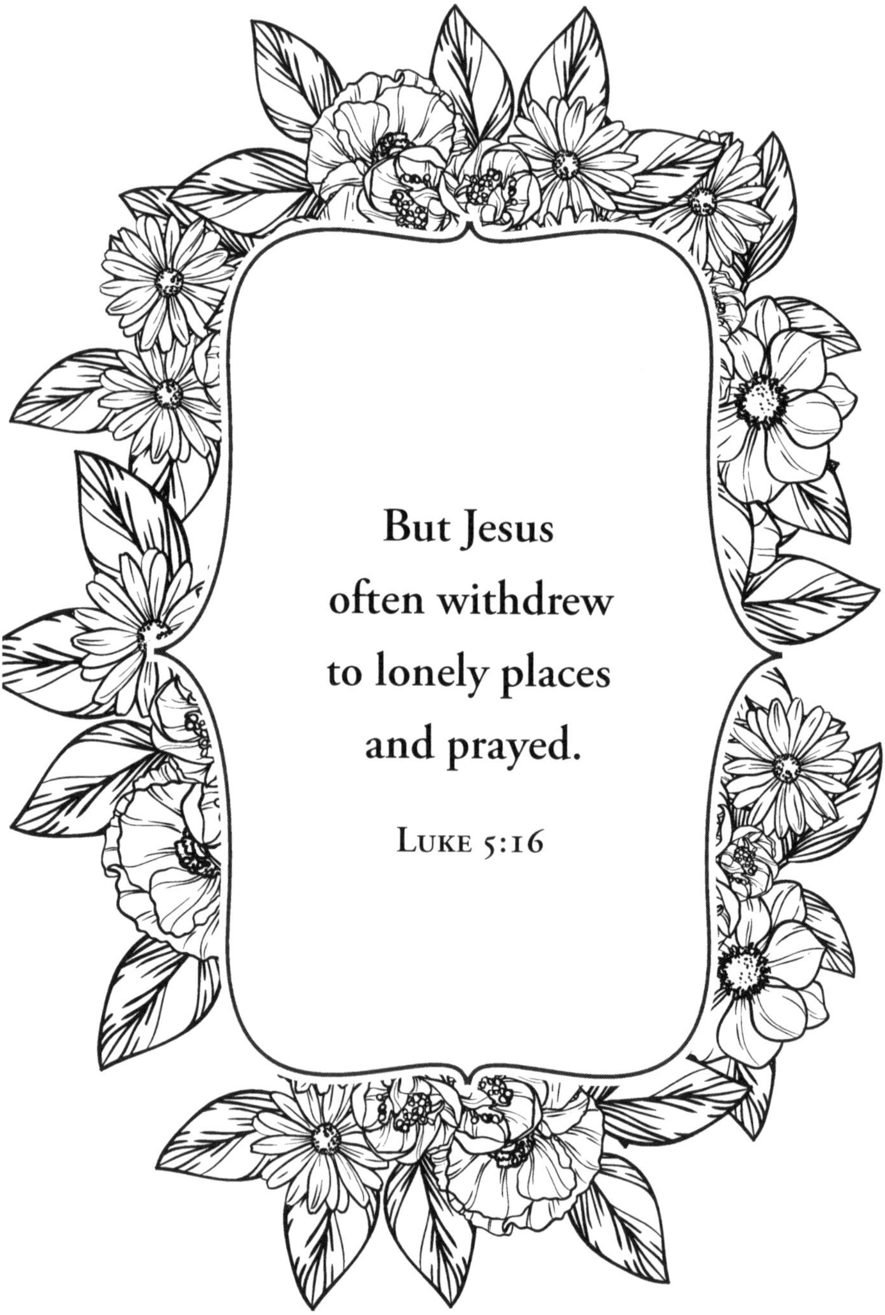

But Jesus often withdrew to lonely places and prayed.

Luke 5:16

Date:

Today I want to remember:

Today I am grateful for:

Prayer

He gives
power to the weak
and strength
to the powerless.

Isaiah 40:29

DATE:

TODAY I WANT TO REMEMBER:

TODAY I AM GRATEFUL FOR:

Prayer

Stay alert! Watch out for your great enemy, the devil. He prowls around like a roaring lion, looking for someone to devour. Stand firm against him, and be strong in your faith. Remember that your family of believers all over the world is going through the same kind of suffering you are. In his kindness God called you to share in his eternal glory by means of Jesus Christ. So after you have suffered a little while, he will restore, support, and strengthen you, and he will place you on a firm foundation. All power to him forever. Amen!

1 Peter 5:8-10

Date:

Today I want to remember:

Today I am grateful for:

Prayer

Show me
the right path,
O Lord;
point out the road
for me to follow.

Psalm 25:4

Date:

Today I want to remember:

Today I am grateful for:

Prayer

**Listen to my voice
in the morning, Lord.
Each morning
I bring my requests to you
and wait expectantly.**

Psalm 5:3

DATE:

TODAY I WANT TO REMEMBER:

TODAY I AM GRATEFUL FOR:

Prayer

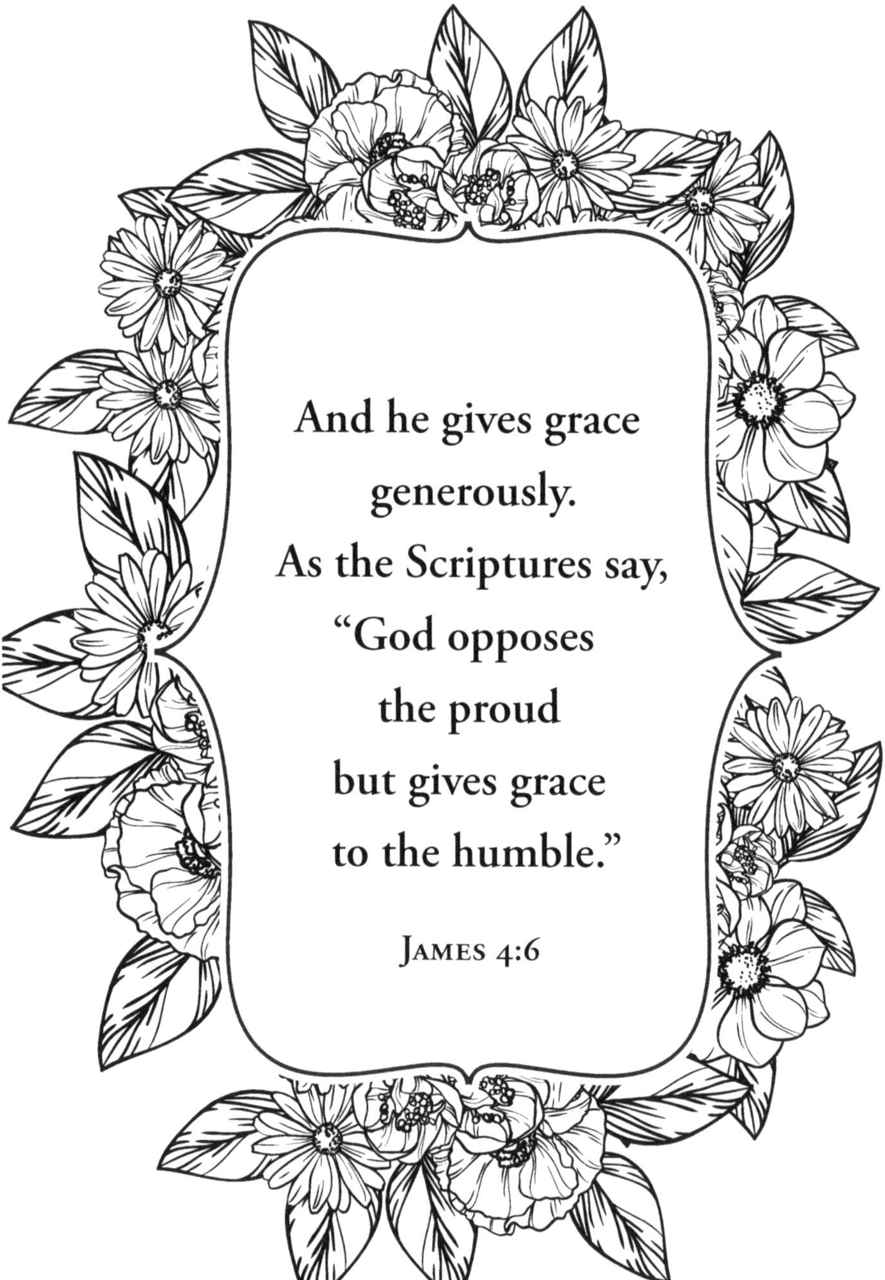

And he gives grace
generously.
As the Scriptures say,
"God opposes
the proud
but gives grace
to the humble."

JAMES 4:6

DATE:

TODAY I WANT TO REMEMBER:

TODAY I AM GRATEFUL FOR:

Prayer

Don't just pretend
to love others.
Really love them.
Hate what is wrong.
Hold tightly to what is good.
Love each other
with genuine affection,
and take delight
in honoring each other.

Romans 12:9-10

Date:

Today I want to remember:

Today I am grateful for:

Prayer

Since God chose you
to be the holy people he loves,
you must clothe yourselves
with tenderhearted mercy,
kindness, humility,
gentleness, and patience.

COLOSSIANS 3:12

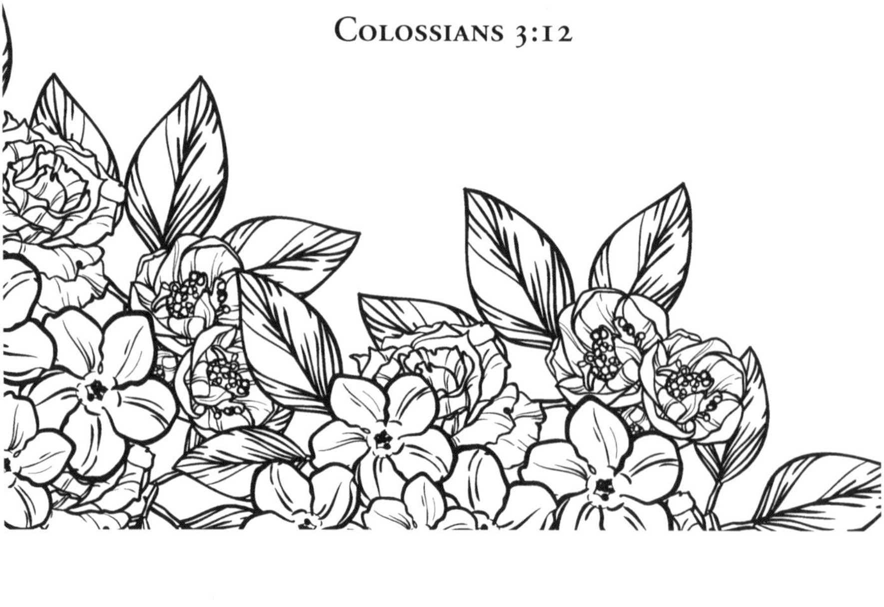

Date:

Today I want to remember:

Today I am grateful for:

Prayer

When you pray,
don't babble on and on
as the Gentiles do.
They think their prayers
are answered merely
by repeating their words
again and again.

Matthew 6:7

DATE:

TODAY I WANT TO REMEMBER:

TODAY I AM GRATEFUL FOR:

Prayer

But when Daniel learned
that the law had been signed,
he went home and knelt down
as usual in his upstairs room,
with its windows open
toward Jerusalem.
He prayed three times a day,
just as he had always done,
giving thanks to his God.

Daniel 6:10

DATE:

TODAY I WANT TO REMEMBER:

TODAY I AM GRATEFUL FOR:

Prayer

The Lord is close
to all who call on him,
yes, to all who call
on him in truth.

Psalm 145:18

DATE:

TODAY I WANT TO REMEMBER:

TODAY I AM GRATEFUL FOR:

Prayer

See that no one
pays back evil for evil,
but always try to
do good to each other
and to all people.
Always be joyful.
Never stop praying.
Be thankful
in all circumstances,
for this is God's will
for you who belong
to Christ Jesus.

1 Thessalonians 5:15-18

DATE:

TODAY I WANT TO REMEMBER:

TODAY I AM GRATEFUL FOR:

Prayer

I love the Lord
because he hears my voice
and my prayer for mercy.
Because he bends down
to listen, I will pray
as long as I have breath!

Psalm 116:1-2

DATE:

TODAY I WANT TO REMEMBER:

TODAY I AM GRATEFUL FOR:

Prayer

**Give thanks to the Lord,
for he is good!
His faithful love
endures forever.**

Psalm 136:1

Date:

Today I want to remember:

Today I am grateful for:

Prayer

**Don’t worry about anything;
instead, pray about everything.
Tell God what you need,
and thank him
for all he has done.**

Philippians 4:6

Date:

Today I want to remember:

Today I am grateful for:

Prayer

Seek the
Kingdom of God
above all else,
and live righteously,
and he will give you
everything you need.

MATTHEW 6:33

Date:

Today I want to remember:

Today I am grateful for:

Prayer

Be still,
and know that I am God!
I will be honored
by every nation.
I will be honored
throughout the world.

Psalm 46:10

DATE:

TODAY I WANT TO REMEMBER:

TODAY I AM GRATEFUL FOR:

Prayer

But the Holy Spirit produces
this kind of fruit in our lives:
love, joy, peace, patience, kindness,
goodness,
faithfulness, gentleness,
and self-control.

Galatians 5:22-23

DATE:

TODAY I WANT TO REMEMBER:

TODAY I AM GRATEFUL FOR:

Prayer

Do everything
without complaining
and arguing.

Philippians 2:14

DATE:

TODAY I WANT TO REMEMBER:

TODAY I AM GRATEFUL FOR:

Prayer

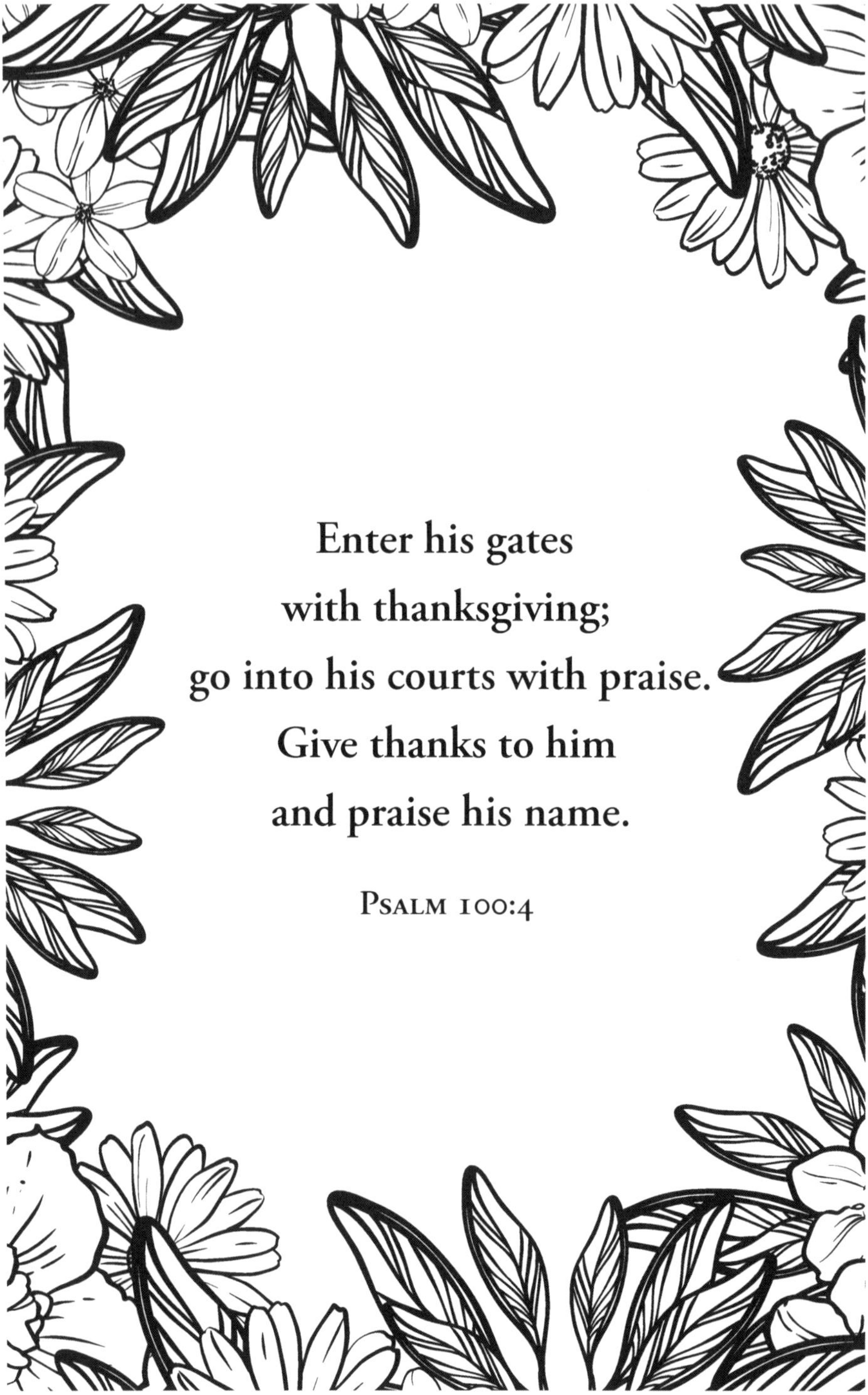

**Enter his gates
with thanksgiving;
go into his courts with praise.
Give thanks to him
and praise his name.**

Psalm 100:4

DATE:

TODAY I WANT TO REMEMBER:

TODAY I AM GRATEFUL FOR:

Prayer

He took some bread and
gave thanks to God for it.
Then he broke it
in pieces and gave it to
the disciples, saying,
"This is my body,
which is given for you.
Do this in
remembrance of me."

LUKE 22:19

DATE:

TODAY I WANT TO REMEMBER:

TODAY I AM GRATEFUL FOR:

Prayer

And we are confident
that he hears us
whenever we ask
for anything
that pleases him.

1 John 5:14

DATE:

TODAY I WANT TO REMEMBER:

TODAY I AM GRATEFUL FOR:

Prayer

And even when you ask,
you don't get it
because your motives
are all wrong,
you want only what
will give you pleasure.

James 4:3

DATE:

TODAY I WANT TO REMEMBER:

TODAY I AM GRATEFUL FOR:

Prayer

Devote yourselves
to prayer with an alert mind
and a thankful heart.

Colossians 4:2

DATE:

TODAY I WANT TO REMEMBER:

TODAY I AM GRATEFUL FOR:

Prayer

Let the message about Christ,
in all its richness,
fill your lives.
Teach and counsel each other
with all the wisdom he gives.
Sing psalms and hymns
and spiritual songs to God
with thankful hearts.

Colossians 3:16

Date:

Today I want to remember:

Today I am grateful for:

Prayer

Obscene stories,
foolish talk,
and coarse jokes,
these are not for you.
Instead, let there be
thankfulness to God.

Ephesians 5:4

DATE:

TODAY I WANT TO REMEMBER:

TODAY I AM GRATEFUL FOR:

Prayer

So now I am giving you
a new commandment:
Love each other.
Just as I have loved you,
you should love each other.
Your love for one another
will prove to the world
that you are my disciples.

John 13:34-35

Date:

Today I want to remember:

Today I am grateful for:

Prayer

All of this is
for your benefit.
And as God's grace
reaches more
and more people,
there will be
great thanksgiving,
and God will receive
more and more glory.

2 Corinthians 4:15

DATE:

TODAY I WANT TO REMEMBER:

TODAY I AM GRATEFUL FOR:

Prayer

And you are helping us
by praying for us.
Then many people will
give thanks because God
has graciously answered
so many prayers for our safety.

2 Corinthians 1:11

DATE:

TODAY I WANT TO REMEMBER:

TODAY I AM GRATEFUL FOR:

Prayer

For God has not given us
a spirit of fear and timidity,
but of power, love,
and self-discipline.

2 Timothy 1:7

DATE:

TODAY I WANT TO REMEMBER:

TODAY I AM GRATEFUL FOR:

Prayer

And let the peace
that comes from Christ
rule in your hearts.
For as members of one body
you are called to live in peace.
And always be thankful.

Colossians 3:15

DATE:

TODAY I WANT TO REMEMBER:

TODAY I AM GRATEFUL FOR:

Prayer

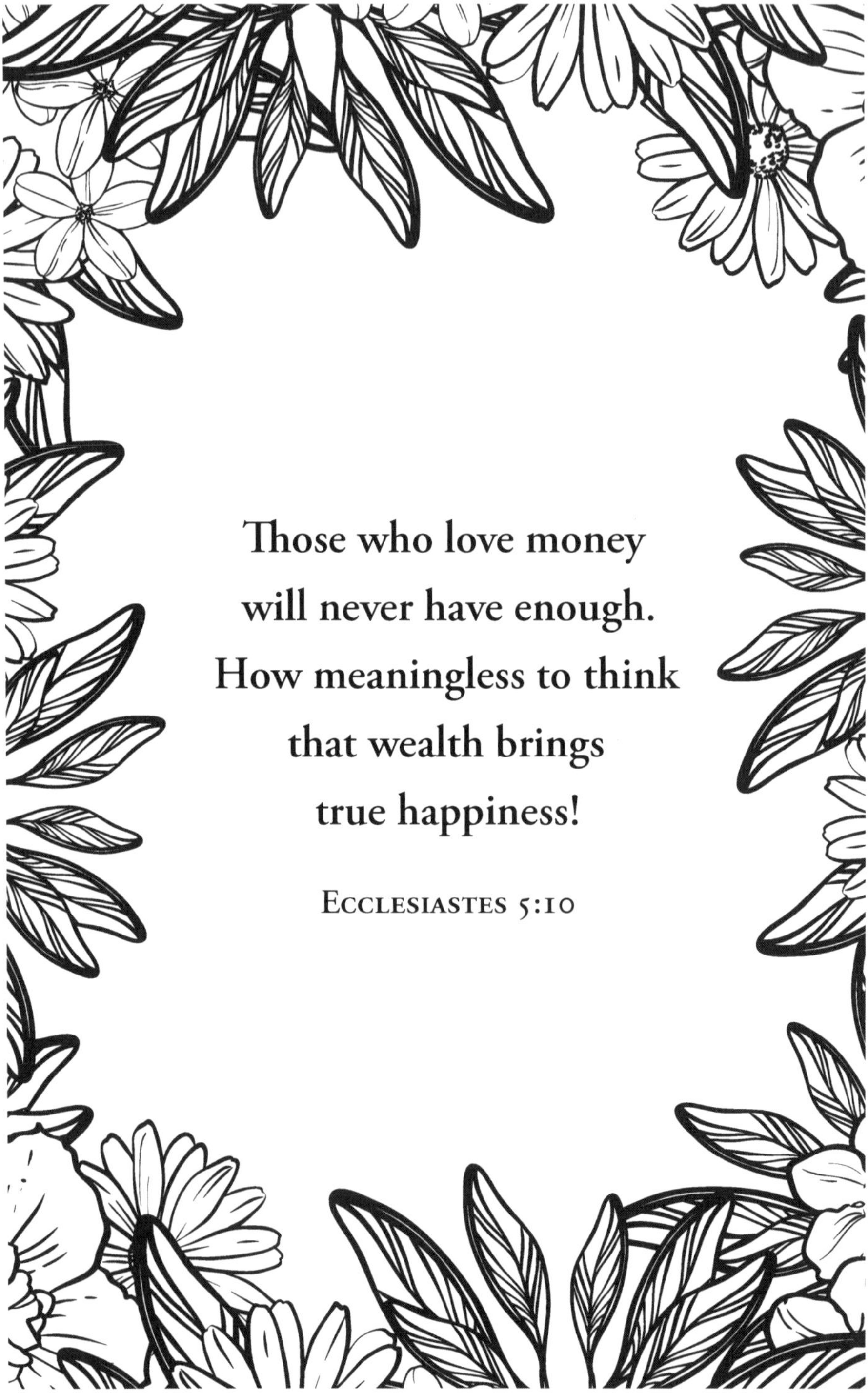

Those who love money
will never have enough.
How meaningless to think
that wealth brings
true happiness!

Ecclesiastes 5:10

DATE:

TODAY I WANT TO REMEMBER:

TODAY I AM GRATEFUL FOR:

Prayer

But I will offer sacrifices
to you with songs of praise,
and I will fulfill all my vows.
For my salvation comes
from the Lord alone.

JONAH 2:9

DATE:

TODAY I WANT TO REMEMBER:

TODAY I AM GRATEFUL FOR:

Prayer

This is the day
the Lord has made.
We will rejoice
and be glad in it.

Psalm 118:24

DATE:

TODAY I WANT TO REMEMBER:

TODAY I AM GRATEFUL FOR:

Prayer

Most important of all,
continue to show deep love
for each other,
for love covers
a multitude of sins.

1 Peter 4:8

DATE:

TODAY I WANT TO REMEMBER:

TODAY I AM GRATEFUL FOR:

Prayer

No, O people,
the Lord has told you
what is good,
and this is what
he requires of you:
to do what is right,
to love mercy,
and to walk humbly
with your God.

Micah 6:8

DATE:

TODAY I WANT TO REMEMBER:

TODAY I AM GRATEFUL FOR:

Prayer

You are
altogether beautiful,
my darling,
beautiful in every way.

Song of Songs 4:7

DATE:

TODAY I WANT TO REMEMBER:

TODAY I AM GRATEFUL FOR:

Prayer

Look at the birds.
They don't plant or harvest or store
food in barns,
for your heavenly Father
feeds them.
And aren't you
far more valuable to him
than they are?
Can all your worries
add a single moment
to your life?

MATTHEW 6:26-27

DATE:

TODAY I WANT TO REMEMBER:

TODAY I AM GRATEFUL FOR:

Prayer

She is clothed with
strength and dignity,
and she laughs without
fear of the future.
When she speaks,
her words are wise,
and she gives instructions
with kindness.

Proverbs 31:25-26

Date:

Today I want to remember:

Today I am grateful for:

Prayer

Connect with Me

Follow and interact with me in these places:

Website and blog: www.GivingGal.com

Facebook: www.facebook.com/GivingGal

Join our Facebook Group: www.facebook.com/groups/givingyourbestlife

Pinterest: Pinterest.com/Giving_Gal

Instagram: @Giving_Gal

LinkedIn: www.linkedin.com/in/StephanieLeeJones

Podcast: Giving Your Best Life (wherever you listen to podcasts)

Children's Books: www.GivingGalBooks.com

I love speaking on giving, gratitude, goals, experiences as a police wife, and leadership. If you need a speaker for your next conference, fundraiser, church service, retreat, school, workshop, or business meeting, I am your gal!

If you have questions, want to share a story, or need giving ideas, drop me an email at Stephanie@GivingGal.com.

I would love to hear from you!

Blessings,

Stephanie

The Perfect Gift

Make a list of people in your life who could benefit from *Thank-You Notes to God* such as a friend, coworker, family member, pastor's wife, women's ministry leader, or your small group. You can purchase copies at www.GivingGal.com/Shop.

Dyslexia Resource

My first book, *The Giving Challenge*, was a labor of love. I never set out to write a book or share my journey. I wanted to make a difference, me as one person to one person each day. What I found was choosing to give daily made a difference to thousands of people. I realized that we could change the world and share positive stories that inspire others to go out and do good.

When I started writing *The Giving Challenge*, I was not a writer. I hated writing. I battled God every day, crying a river of tears. I quit numerous times, and that's why it took four to five years to publish the first edition. I did not want to write that book. Period. Not only did I hate writing, but when I did write, it was terrible. I had poor grammar. And I can't spell worth a darn. But with all those excuses, I learned to be obedient and not rely on my strengths but to trust in God and have faith.

Right before I released *The Giving Challenge*, I received a dyslexia diagnosis. A weight I carried for years lifted off my shoulders in an instant. As I shared in this book, I struggled most of my life in silence. But something happened after I sent my first book out into the world. I fell in love with writing.

A water hose of stories and book ideas have flooded my mind ever since. It's my sincere hope that if you've read both of my books, you'll see improvement in my writing. Because like anything, if we work at the craft, we can improve. I now attend writer's conferences and work with great editors to learn and grow. I even dream of speaking at writer's conferences, sharing my journey with other writers to encourage them to take a step of faith and share their stories with the world.

If you have book in you but don't know where to start, I'm here to help. Reach out to me at Stephanie@GivingGal.com, and let's chat about the next step you need to take to see your book on a bookshelf.

P.S. I shared my dyslexia story with you as you may have dyslexia and do not know it. Or maybe you do know and need a little encouragement. Perhaps there is a child in your life who finds reading and writing challenging. Do not ignore them. They are smart. He only needs to learn differently. Get him help. If you don't know where to start, connect with my dear friend Joellyn Hartley at www.JoellynHartley.com. She changed my life and I know she can do the same for you or a child in your life.

Acknowledgments

I love journals! It is a dream come true to create a journal and share it with you. The more I write and spend time in the Word of God, the more I realize none of this work is mine, but His. He gave me the journal idea and title. I am faithful in acting on what He called me to do. I challenge you to do the same.

Special thanks to:

Mike, my husband—thanks for always supporting my crazy ideas. I love you!

Rebekah—your creativity always brings my ideas to life. Somehow you can interpret what I think and make it ten times better. I do not know what I would do without you as my partner in crime at Giving Gal.

My friends who were willing to beta the journal for me. This journal is the best product I could publish because of the generous feedback from Cortney, Becky, Whitney, Rebecca, Emily, Donna, Jasman, Melissa, Nicoya, Najee, and Kerrie.

The Giving Your Best Life Facebook group friends that contributed their favorite verses. Thank you to Cara, Jeni, Harold, Nate, Cortney, Nancy M., Robin, Lisa, Nancy D., Kathy, Laurie, Timeko, and Jessica.

My friends, Bethany, and Michelle, at Platinum Literary Service. I am so grateful God connected us first on social media and then in person. I could not put this journal out into the world without you.

My amazing editor Crystal Humble. My books are reader-worthy because of you.

My readers, faithful followers, family, and friends—thank you from the bottom of my heart for all your love, support, and big cheers from the sidelines. There is never a minute I forget it is because of you I can live out my dream and consider myself a successful author. I love you all!